Paul VI

by
Anthony Symondson SJ

All booklets are published thanks to the generous support of the members of the Catholic Truth Society

CATHOLIC TRUTH SOCIETY
PUBLISHERS TO THE HOLY SEE

Contents

Introduction

On 25th July 1968 Pope Paul VI promulgated the encyclical, *Humanae Vitae*, 'Of Human Life'. Many regard this document as the most prophetic of his encyclicals for the way that it foretold the consequences of taking the conception of life lightly and the diminution this would have on human society. Pope Benedict XVI declared at a conference in Rome marking the fortieth anniversary of *Humanae Vitae* that, 'The truth of *Humanae Vitae* does not change; rather, in the light of the new scientific findings, its teaching becomes ever more up-to-date and induces reflection on its intrinsic value.'

This anniversary provides an opportunity to look at the life and achievement of Giovanni Battista Montini (1897-1978) who reigned as Paul VI from 1963 until 1978. Peter Hebblethwaite, Pope Paul's English biographer (to whose work this study is deeply indebted) described him as the 'first modern Pope' and that is an accurate description. Battista Montini was consistently a man of his time and the theological discourse, political controversies and social development of the twentieth century - locally in Italy, more widely in Europe, the United States and the emerging nations of the Third World - engaged his time and attention as a Vatican diplomat in the department of the Secretary of State and later as Pope.

Above all, Paul was the Pope of the 21st Ecumenical Council of the Roman Catholic Church, known as the Second Vatican Council. Convened by Blessed Pope John XXIII in 1959, held from 1962-5, it was Paul who guided the Council for the greater part of its proceedings, implemented the Council's decrees in the aftermath, and consciously tried to move the Church to meet the demands of modernity. He was involved in the strands of development before the Council that flowed into its deliberations and their application in the aftermath.

Paul was the first Pope in modern times to travel, first to the Holy Land, the source of the Christian faith; to the United States, where he restored the prestige of the Church in international affairs; to India, a great non-Christian religious nation, and to many other countries. In this he anticipated the world travel of Pope John Paul II and both made possible the present travel of Pope Benedict XVI. In his time the Papacy became an institution of ever greater, universal significance.

During Paul's reign of fifteen years more changes were introduced in the Church than in all previous centuries combined. These included the promulgation of a new Roman Missal, the translation of the Roman Rite into the vernacular, the reform of the Roman Curia, and the amplification of the Sacred College of Cardinals to represent more fully the Church's international character. His great achievement was to put the Catholic Church and the Papacy itself into the centre of the world stage. His pontificate defined the Papacy's new role and he had safeguarded the substance of the Catholic faith intact.

Naturally diffident and shy, this was achieved at considerable spiritual and personal cost. For most of his life he had indifferent health, feeling, for much of the time, neither well nor ill. The cross and suffering were at the centre of Paul's affective life but, above all, he remained a dedicated priest during his entire adult life: as a Vatican diplomat, Cardinal-Archbishop of Milan, and Supreme Pontiff of the Universal Church, and he regarded the exercise of authority in the Church as a service, not an honour.

Anthony Symondson SJ
Farm Street 2008

A simple funeral

In the month of June 1963, an unusual phenomenon occurred in London. Quite spontaneously, in all directions, the buildings flew their flags at half-mast for the death of Pope John XXIII. This response had not previously occurred on the death of a pope in the modern history of Britain. Pope John, a man of radiant humanity, had transformed the Papacy from being the exclusive preserve of the Roman Catholic Church to an institution recognised universally as a force for good. Catholics, Protestants and non-Christian religions began to look at the Church with new eyes and this was due entirely to the force of personality of good Pope John. The world as a whole mourned the loss of a spiritual leader.

Fifteen years later, on the Feast of the Transfiguration, 6th August 1978, Pope Paul VI, his successor, died at the age of eighty at Castelgandolfo, the papal summer villa in the district of Lazio, in the Alban hills, thirty miles from Rome. Flags were flown to mark his death but the public response was muted. Paul possessed none of the charismatic charm manifested by his predecessor. He was quiet, shy, introspective, undemonstrative, private, bookish, an intellectual, and for most of his life he had been an official in the Roman Curia; the Vatican was his second home. But his funeral, five days later on 11th August, not only characterised the man but also the dramatic changes in the Catholic Church over which he had presided during his reign. Paul's instructions broke with tradition. Previously it had been the custom to bury the Pope as if he were a Renaissance prince. Paul directed that his funeral should be 'pious and simple'. This was the first papal funeral to be held in St Peter's Square and was striking in its starkness. The plain coffin rested on the ground, rather than on an elaborate catafalque. Instead of the papal tiara, a mitre, or even a stole, all that stood on the coffin's lid was an open book of the Gospels, the pages lightly moving in the breeze. He said that he wanted his body to be buried in the bare earth and that there should be no monument.

Pope Paul VI reigned over the Catholic Church during most of the Second Vatican Council and played a central role in implementing its decrees. Pope John XXIII inaugurated the Council in 1962 and died at the end of the first session in the following year. The proceedings continued until 1965. No event had a more radical effect on the modern Church, and no pope was left a more difficult legacy by his predecessor. Few twentieth-century popes have been eclipsed more completely than Paul VI but none were more decisive in shaping the future. Overshadowed by his predecessors and successors, his life has lessons for all and looking at it will help many understand the present time.

Early life and family background

Giovanni Battista Enrico Antonio Maria Montini was born in Concesio, in the province of Brescia, Lombardy, in northern Italy, on 26th September 1897. He was the second son of Giorgio Montini, a prosperous, non-practicing lawyer and landowner who was also editor of the local Catholic newspaper, *Il Cittadino di Brescia*, and a parliamentary deputy with a strong desire for social reform. Giuditta Alghisi, his mother, was a rich orphan from a family of local nobles and a leader of the Catholic women of Brescia. Their first son, Lodovico, was born in 1896, their third, Francesco, in 1900. The family originated in the Alps at Valsabbia (or possibly Savallese) but in the fifteenth century came down to the city below. Originally their surname was Benedetti or de Benedictus. Montini was a handle that stuck and they remained the people of the mountains.

Brescia was defined by mountains. Bounded to east and west by Lakes Garda and Iseo, to the north by the rich dairy lands of the Alps and the south by the fertile Po valley it was marked out by an idyllic self-sufficiency. Its industrial wealth since the Renaissance was based on steel, arms and armour. In 1981 Lodovico Montini declared that the province of Brescia was a microcosm of

Italy and it is still regarded as the political barometer of the country. Georgio Montini worked hard as an editor to include Italian Catholics in national politics. They had been excluded by the papal *non expedit* which said that they should be 'neither electors nor elected'. Encouraged by the policies of Pope Leo XIII - an old man who rejuvenated the Church, opened the Vatican archives and declared that the Church had nothing to fear from the truth (he reigned between 1878 and 1903) - these ambitions were repressed on the election of Cardinal Guiseppe Sarto, Patriarch of Venice, in 1903. Pope Pius X timidly returned to the isolationist policies of Pope Pius IX, who wore the tiara from 1846 until 1878 and in whose reign the temporal power of the Pope decreased, until, in 1907, the *non expedit* was lifted because the Pope feared that Italy would turn socialist. These early influences were to bear fruit in the adult life of Battista Montini.

Jesuit education

In 1903, at the age of six, Montini started school at the Jesuit Collegio Cesare Arici. Georgio Montini had campaigned for the right of Catholics to set up private schools in Brescia and had helped to found the school in 1888. He sent his three sons there and the family lived at via Trieste 37, in the same street; Montini could see the college from his bedroom window. He was a delicate, pious, if spirited, child, made to sit in the front row of his class, and was taught by lay masters and mistresses. His contact with the Society of Jesus was slight until he moved on to the upper school and was taught by Jesuits. The Jesuit education of those days was formal but systematic and the discipline thorough. In the summer of 1914, at the age of sixteen, Montini's parents decided that he should leave the Arici because of his fragile health and finish his education privately, taking his exams at the state high school, Arnaldo da Brescia. Before doing so Montini had assumed a high place in the Sodality of Our Lady, preached his first sermons as a layman in the Sodality Chapel, and was described as the 'soul' of the Sodality when he eventually left in 1917.

Oratorian parish influence

Spiritually he and his brothers were more deeply influenced by the Oratorians. The Montini family worshipped at the church of Sant' Antonio de la Pace in Brescia, the Oratorian parish. The arrival in 1912 of two young priests in their thirties, Giulio Bevilacqua and Paulo Caresana, had an enormous influence on the parish and upon the Montini brothers in particular. Bevilacqua had a doctorate in social sciences from the University of Louvain on Italian law and the Workers. He saw the link between the Church's social teaching and the liturgy and made La Pace a model for parish liturgy. The Oratorians had attracted him by their freedom of spirit. In 1965

Montini, as Pope Paul VI, made Bevilacqua a cardinal at the age of 85, partly in recognition of his broadening influence on him when young. Bevilacqua accepted the honour on condition that he could stay as parish priest in a working-class suburb of Brescia and retain the black cassock. He had taught Montini to read the signs of the Holy Spirit in the modern world and he remained his 'master and friend' until his death weeks later.

Signs of a vocation

Paulo Caresana became Montini's confessor and spiritual director and remained so until Caresana's death in 1973. He introduced him to apostolic works and, on the outbreak of war, employed him as his unpaid secretary. His influence was profound but cannot be gauged as clearly as Bevilacqua's because of its confidential nature. Montini was a keen bicyclist and both priests shared his passion. Some read this enthusiasm as evidence of 'modernism' and the Jesuits did not approve of the Oratorians' openness to friendship. But the humanity of Bevilacqua and Caresana, in association with Georgio Montini's social ideals, formed Montini the priest, bishop, cardinal and pope in ways which none imagined at the time.

Montini's best friend at school was Andrea Trebeschi. On St Andrew's day, 30th November 1914, when they were both seventeen, Trebeschi invited him to write a page in his diary. Beneath the entry he wrote:

> Battista Montini, my good friend, wrote this memento in my book. What a wonderful soul he has! What an example his life is, inspired entirely by the good; what a precious and dear warning is conveyed in his words! He is offering his life to God: *he is going to be a priest.* We will always be friends.

This was the first intimation that Montini wanted to be a priest. There had been no signs of a vocation in his early boyhood but several influences contributed to the desire for a priestly life.

The war and the seminary

The outbreak of war in August 1914 effected delays in Montini's pursuit of his vocation. Italy entered the war in 1915 and it was not until 1916 that he began studies for the diocesan priesthood. These were unconventional. As a prospective seminarian he was exempt from conscription. By special dispensation he became an external student and was allowed to live and study at home and attend lectures as often as he could. The seminary of Sant' Angelo was requisitioned as a storehouse for a military hospital and the number of seminarians had been depleted by the war. By 1917 they were reduced to Montini and one other but when war ended the seminary gradually filled up. It was a lonely start. Father Caresana remained close: 'His fatherhood was my seminary', Montini succinctly recalled. During his years there he, with Andrea Trebeschi and his father, visited Rome. He found it hard to pray 'amid the pomp and ceremony' and preferred the Catacombs. He met Cardinal Achille Ratti, Prefect of the Vatican Library (later Pope Pius XI), and his father, after an audience with Pope Benedict XV, emerged as the President of the Unione Populare, the direct ancestor of the Christian Democrats.

Priest at twenty two

As he approached ordination he sought solitude on a retreat at Monte Cassino. He was enchanted by the Abbey and believed that should a new dark age descend upon Europe, Benedictine abbeys, above all Monte Cassino, would assume their traditional role as guardians of civilisation. 'After Rome,' he wrote to his father, 'I believe no other shrine evokes so strongly the Christian tradition, and makes self-evident the desire not to be unworthy of it, but to be among its humble, alert and convinced continuators'. It was his last retreat before embarking on the minor orders which led to priestly ordination. He was tonsured on 30th November 1919, became a doorkeeper and lector on 14th December, was raised to the sub-diaconate on 28th February 1920, ordained to the diaconate on 8th March and to the priesthood, at the age of twenty-two, on 29th May. His mother, Giuditta, had her wedding dress made into a set of white vestments and Montini celebrated his first Mass in the Sanctuary of the Madonna delle Grazie in Brescia on the following day. His ordination card had a copy of Rubens's *Last Supper* and this prayer: 'Grant, oh my God, that all minds may unite in the Truth, and all hearts in Charity.' It contained an indulgence of 300 days given by Pope Pius X.

Montini's Bishop, Giacinto Gaggia, decided to send him for further studies in literature at Rome's Sapienza University, after which he would do a doctorate in history. Rome now became his milieu and home. He was conscientious at his studies but the results were mixed and conditions at the Lombardy college were primitive. He was taken up as a protégé by his father's friend, Giovanni Longinotti, Under-Secretary to the Ministry of Commerce and Labour, became an honorary uncle to his children, and baptised them as they came along. Longinotti frequently dined with Cardinal Piero Gasparri, Secretary of State. He suggested that Montini was languishing at the Lombardy College and that he would be better off at the Academy for Noble Ecclesiastics, the school for Vatican diplomats. Wheels turned.

Diplomatic career

He was summoned by Msgr Guiseppe Pizzardo, substitute to the Secretary of State, on 27th October 1921 and told to be ready to enter the Academy. He neither sought, nor wanted, a diplomatic career but with the influences of Church and State bearing down upon him he had no option. A fortnight later Battista Montini entered the Academy of Noble Ecclesiastics in the Piazza Minerva and began to study canon law with the Jesuits at the Gregorian University. He felt trapped and he spent an entire hour one afternoon sewing buttons on his cassock, and joked: 'To be well buttoned up is an essential characteristic of the diplomatic life.' He was also unhappy with the canonical approach to life and wondered whether it was possible to translate the Gospel into terms of canon law: 'The further one is from the external forms of the Gospel, the more one must insist on the *spirit*, but since the practice of the paradoxical Christian virtues is difficult enough, it is almost impossible to practice them by means that are contrary to their very nature.' He was mistrustful of the Academy from the outset.

Change of Pope

On 22nd January 1922, Pope Benedict XV died of pneumonia. With the Roman crowds sheltering under a sea of umbrellas beneath a tormented sky, Montini visited the body laid out in the Blessed Sacrament Chapel of St Peter's. He caught influenza and on his sick bed he sketched a portrait, drawn from his daily mediation on the Gospels, of what a pope should be:

> The Church is about to be embodied in a man who after twenty centuries should represent not only the powerful Christ but the Christ who is evangelical, peace-loving, holy and poor. Let us pray that we may merit a pope who is very like Jesus; and for that he will have to be crucified by the world that hates what is not its own; its salvation demands as much.

Pope Benedict was succeeded by Cardinal Achille Ratti, Archbishop of Milan, on 6th February 1922, who took the name of Pius XI. Tough-minded, unyielding and vigorous in defence of the institutional rights of the Church, he was a good choice to confront the world in the emerging age of dictators.

First journeys abroad

At that time, Montini underwent moments of depression associated with poor health but he passed his second-year canon law examination with relief. He left Rome on 1st July 1922 for Austria and Germany to learn German and in his absence Benito Mussolini became Prime Minister. He disliked German art, saw the Oberammagau Passion Play, witnessed the hyper-inflation of the country, and took a steamer down the Rhine from Mainz to Bonn. Then, in October, he was ordered by Msgr Pizzardo, to complete his canon law studies as soon as possible. These he accomplished at home in Brescia and he was awarded a doctorate in December. He expressed a desire to return to his diocese. Then, in January 1923, Pizzardo told him he should hold himself ready to enter the Secretariat of State and declared, 'with breath-taking naiveté', that he should steel himself to go to Poland or Peru or possibly Hungary as an attaché where he would have no other duty than to 'observe how a nunciature works'. He restated his desire to return to Brescia. By 5th June 1923 Montini was in Vienna on his way to Poland.

Poland as a nation state was barely five years old when Battista Montini arrived in Warsaw in the torrid summer heat. Only one bridge across the Vistula was usable, the Poniatowski Bridge lay in ruins after the Russian attack of August 1920 and the Russian Orthodox Cathedral was destroyed shortly after he arrived. The national situation was complicated, relations with Rome were bad, and Montini had great difficulty in learning Polish. Msgr Carlo Chiarlo, an official who took charge during the absence of the Nuncio, Bishop Lorenzo Lauri - well knowing the hazardous nature of Vatican appointments - argued with Pizzardo that Montini should not remain in Poland, since its cruel winter would ruin his already fragile health. He recommended that his gifted subordinate should continue academic work. Georgio Montini tried to exert influence to have his son returned to Italy but the Pope decided that he should stay in Warsaw. Then, unexpectedly, on 2nd October a telegram arrived from the Secretary of State, Cardinal Gasparri. It read: 'MONTINI AUTHORISED RETURN ROME'. 'Thus concludes,' Montini wrote in a private note, 'This episode of my life which has provided useful though not always joyful experiences, from which only later and with maturity I may profit according to the designs of Providence.'

Were these months wasted? He had learnt to read the map of Poland, could visualise scenes of future wartime horrors, understand the millennium celebrations of 1966 (which took place in the fourth year of his pontificate) and appreciate the international scene of Karol Wojtyla, successor of Cardinal Adam Sapieha, in Krakow. Montini was back at the Pontifical Academy by 12th October 1923 and embarked upon his Roman apprenticeship in the Secretariat of State, at the age of twenty-six, as 'ecclesiastical assistant', or chaplain, to the Catholic students of Rome. Thus began his thirty-one years of service in the Secretariat.

Work in the Secretariat of State

The Church's main task was to cope with the new Fascist regime. The Federazione degli Universita Cattolica Italiano (FUCI) was in political turmoil. FUCI was part of Catholic Action, a movement of Catholic laity started by Pius X and actively supported by Pius XI. The Fascists were sweeping all before them and FUCI was the only serious opposition to them in the university. It was a dangerous time, complicated by the Church's desire to solve, once and for all, the Roman question which had resulted from the fall of the city of Rome as the last territory of the Papal States in 1870. This was resolved by the Lateran Treaty between the Church and the Italian government in 1929 but the negotiations inevitably involved compromise and appeasement and put Montini into difficulties in his new role. He had to meet the needs of Catholics who for the first time in their lives found themselves invited to choose between an anti-Christian ideology and a personally appropriated Christian faith.

Chaplain to Catholic students

For the next seven years he trod delicate ground. Montini spent the mornings at the Pontifical Academy and the late afternoon and evenings at the chaplaincy. He recovered the use of the parish church of Sant' Ivo for students, organised retreats for them at the basilica of St Paul-Without-the-Walls, and conducted weekly visits of their conference of the Society of St Vincent de Paul to anticlerical slum areas in and near Rome. It was difficult to find neutral, non-partisan topics of discussion at meetings; almost everything could be given a political twist. His influence was exercised in deepening the spiritual, liturgical and intellectual life of the students. Influenced by Romano Guardini, the Italo-German priest, philosopher and intellectual, later Professor of Philosophy at Munich, he taught the need to grasp the inner meaning of the liturgy:

> A good liturgy does not consist in the correct observance of the rubrics and the rules; it involves the Christian soul and calls it really to take part in this act of adoration and homage to God. This is what the Church intends. It is not enough to follow the ceremonies with physical eyes, one needs to plumb them with the deepest spiritual sense. It is a waste of time to be present at Catholic worship unless the soul reaches out beyond the gestures and externals.

Montini much admired Guardini's pioneering work, *The Spirit of the Liturgy* (1922). His language anticipated Pope Pius XII's encyclical, *Mediator Dei*, which emphasised 'active participation' in the liturgy and the enthusiasm of Pope Benedict XVI for Guardini's work. Other writers who influenced him at this time were Maurice Zundel, a Swiss priest, Georges Bernanos, the French novelist, Jacques Maritain and Étienne Gilson, the French Thomist philosophers. As pope he quoted Zundel's lapidary, 'God is not an invention but a discovery,' and invited him to give the annual retreat to the Roman Curia in 1972. Karl Adam's *The Spirit of Catholicism* (1924) left a permanent mark on his theological thinking. Jean Guitton, the French philosopher and theologian, became a friend.

With his appointment as chaplain, Montini had at last secured a proper job, though only on the lowest rung of the curial ladder. His entire future depended on this move. The new intake at the Secretariat also included Alfredo Ottaviani, already famous for his lectures on canon law at the Lateran. In 1925 Montini became a domestic prelate, assigned to the second section of the Secretariat which dealt with foreign governments as *minutante*. His superior was Cardinal Gasparri, Secretary of State, but he also had to deal with Msgr Duca, Secretary for Extraordinary Affairs, Msgr Pizzardo, *sostitito*, Domenico Spada, Chancellor of Apostolic Briefs, and Pietro Cariaci, Under-Secretary for Extraordinary Affairs. Of his colleagues in 1925 Pizzardo, Ottaviani and Ciriaci, would all be present at the conclave in 1963 in which he became Pope.

Political turmoil

Trouble broke when Montini was denounced to Pius XI for allowing Catholic Action to be used for political ends. He had organised a week of social studies, addressed by his brother Lodovico, to commemorate Pope Leo XIII's encyclical, *Rerum Novarum*. He explained that some of the students were interested in political matters and wished to be involved in them but the lectures were purely historical without any political implications; this absolved his superiors from any responsibility. But the result was that on 11th June, the feast of Corpus Christi, a gang of Fascists belaboured with truncheons a group of his own students as they processed towards the Porta Pia. Next day Catholic students were savagely assaulted as they went about the university. The message was that there was room only for a Fascist student movement.

Montini vainly tried to resign but he was, instead, appointed national chaplain to FUCI and remained in this post for a further eight years. It was a difficult post. In 1925 all political parties except the Fascists were dissolved; all democratic associations or groups were outlawed; and there were arrests and deportations without trial. Montini took charge of the Catholic student movement throughout Italy. Accidentally, at the age of twenty-eight, he became the covert leader of the intellectual opposition to the Fascists. From 1926 to 1933 FUCI, a potentially dissident movement, was the only serious opposition in the university with Montini as its leader. During these years Catholic student congresses he organised were broken up by Fascist students, his father's newspaper was banned and the printing presses destroyed.

Montini founded a weekly newspaper, *La Sapienza*, to develop a militantly Catholic intellectual élite, and he contributed many articles both to this periodical and to the bulletin *Azione Fucina*. In 1927 he and Igino Righetti, the national president of FUCI, founded a small publishing house, Studium; and Montini became editor, and main contributor, to the monthly intellectual review, *Studium*. They raised the standards, increased the circulation, and moved the place of publication from Bologna to Rome; they developed the programme and the organisation of FUCI through study groups, regional conventions and national congresses. He believed that intellectual activity was in itself deeply spiritual and was inspired by the French Dominican periodical, *La Vie Intellectuelle*, which developed a spirituality of intellectual work. Research was to be done in an atmosphere of dialogue. Friendship was an intellectual virtue, and not merely an escape from loneliness. He came to adopt the position of the French lay professors, Etienne Gilson and Jacques Maritain, who went back to the original texts of Aquinas, to that of the neo-scholastics for whom Thomism was an all-embracing, self-sufficient system. Maritain was destined to have a great influence on Italian Catholicism and Montini translated his *Three Reformers* for Italian readers.

Bitterness of failure

In Italy the attacks on Catholic Action intensified in the spring of 1931. All FUCI congresses were cancelled. On

29th May all Catholic youth movements in Italy, FUCI specifically included, were dissolved and their property confiscated. It was the bitterest day of Montini's life so far. On 31st May the headquarters at Piazza Sant' Agostino were surrounded by Fascist police. Within, FUCI students recited the rosary in semi-darkness. FUCI premises were violently attacked in Venice, Florence, Milan and Genoa. 'From all over Italy,' he wrote home, 'there comes the discreet and grieving lamentation of our devastated groups.' Montini and Righetti suspended public gatherings of the federation but continued to conduct private meetings.

Pius XI reacted with a vigorous encyclical, *Non abbiamo bisogno* (We do not need this), promulgated on 7th July. It was diffused abroad so that it would be known even if the Fascists banned it in Italy. The encyclical was ambivalent. It denounced the regime for its 'out-and-out pagan worship of the state', and for educating Italian youth 'in hatred, violence, and even irreverence towards the Pope himself'. What most upset the Fascists was the papal recommendation that the Fascist oath could be taken provided one added the mental reservation, 'saving the laws of God and the Church, or saving the duties of a good Christian'. At the same time it did not rule out hopes of an accommodation: 'We do not wish to condemn the Party and the regime as such, but we do mean to draw attention to policies that are contrary to Catholic theory and practise.'

When Mussolini visited the Vatican in 1932 he made it clear that relations between Italy and the Holy See would improve if Montini were forbidden to have future contact with student groups. On 9th March 1933 he received a letter from Msgr Pizzardo, head of Catholic Action, curtly informing him that he was relieved of his post as national chaplain of FUCI. He was dismissed and thanked at the same time. The reason given was that his work at the Secretariat of State was now so important that it demanded his full-time attention. Montini had wanted to resign from the Secretariat in order to concentrate on the student chaplaincy, work which seemed more urgent. This was not an argument calculated to appeal to Pius XI. 'Msgr Montini', he replied, 'has gifts destined to permit him to render service to the Church on a much higher level.' He could not disguise his disappointment and regarded the Pope's decision as a station along the *Via Crucis*.

Pastoral character

In 1930 Cardinal Gasparri was succeeded as Secretary of State by Cardinal Eugenio Pacelli. Pacelli was tall, thin, ascetic, and princely in bearing: an exacting perfectionist and relentless taskmaster, a curialist to his fingertips. For four years previously he had been Nuncio in Berlin. He had little sympathy for Montini's chaplaincy work and could not hide his amazement that Montini was involved in matters so remote from his official duties, despite the fact that he had been given the work by Msgr Pizzardo, a decision confirmed by the Pope. Pacelli saw the question in bureaucratic terms and so did Montini's immediate superiors, Ottaviano and Pizzardo. They dismissed the matter as a storm in a teacup and did not understand why he cared about FUCI and the young people among whom he had worked so conscientiously. But in 1932 Montini collaborated in the founding of the Movimento Laureati Cattolici for the continuation of this apostolate among university graduates; and in 1936 he helped to organise the 'Seminars of Camaldoli', from which leaders of the Christian Democratic Party emerged after the collapse of Fascism.

His rule of life

Montini's dismissal as chaplain to FUCI caused a crisis of conscience and integrity. His most urgent problem was how to lead a Christian life in the midst of careerists. During a retreat at Monte Cassino in 1930 he had resolved 'To choose the humblest offices in the Church, because they are closest to the kingdom. Not to aim to have a career; to prefer the apostle to the canon lawyer;

the parish priest to the cathedral canon or religious; the missionary to the bureaucrat; the teacher to the scholar.' But he had offices thrust upon him and was not allowed to follow this humble path. He had anticipated this inevitability and during the retreat he established a principle to which he would remain faithful for the rest of his life - including his pontificate:

> *Authority* in the Church is a service, not an honour. Vanity plays an important part here, also within the Church; one should not encourage it, still less make it one's own. When one has an office one should (1) carry it out with firmness and courage; neither being depressed or crawling; one should not confine one's actions merely to what is possible but should try, dare and risk doing as much good as possible. All evasions - whether out of laziness or exhaustion - go against the Holy Spirit. Mental desertion is not allowed; reasonable abstention is. One should therefore learn how to give orders, and how to put up with the unsuccessful results of one's efforts. (2) One should study the real needs of people and the works on which one is engaged, and try to meet them. One should feel the sufferings of others, and the suffering in others, and uncover the resources of good that God has placed in souls, or at least to try to discover them.

Such were his principles: to do the good one can within the limitations of office.

One result of Montini's transformation into a reluctant full-time bureaucrat was that he became almost invisible. He was immersed in curial work and became a technician whose task was to draft and redraft documents to the satisfaction of Cardinal Pacelli and his chief assistant, Msgr Ottaviani. They were both sticklers who wanted executants rather than collaborators. Pope Pius XI was obstinate, fussy, pedantic, given to unaccountable rages and thought of as a modern man. Montini stood is awe of him. The main diplomatic activity of his pontificate consisted in making concordats. Montini became a workaholic confined within the Vatican but he took seriously his teaching of diplomatic history at the Pontifical Academy and in order to relieve the intensity of desk-work he took up charitable works and occasional travel. He worked in Primavalle, a poor quarter of Rome, where he led the local St Vincent de Paul Society. In this way he came to the aid of those whom the Fascist regime regarded as hopeless.

Reluctant promotion

On 13th December 1937 Montini was appointed substitute to the Secretariat of State. His promotion to be assistant to Cardinal Pacelli was a sign of the Vatican's growing disillusionment with Fascism. He took over from Domenico Tardini, who became Secretary to the Extraordinary Affairs Section, which dealt with governments. At forty, Battista Montini was now, in effect, the chief executive officer to the Secretary of State. He became a consulter to the Holy Office, which vetted orthodoxy, and of the Consistorial Congregation, which vetted future bishops, Secretary to the Cipher and a member of the Signatura, the Supreme Court. There is evidence that he tried to decline his new post. Rumours had reached home but were pacified when Fr Caresana, his Oratorian confessor, sent a telegram to his parents, 'EDIFYING RESISTANCE FINALLY OVERCOME'. His new apartment was in the Apostolic Palace and he remained living within the Vatican for the next seventeen years, his longest stay at any one place.

Despite his new influence, Montini's manner did not change. He treated his employees as human beings, his fellow-priests as brothers, he had the gift of making visitors feel they were the most important people in the world. He tried to lead a Christian life in the Curia, saw his work as a form of apostolate, he lived simply and preferred the tram to the official car. He heard confessions in Sant' Anna and stayed in touch with the St Vincent de Paul Conference at Primavalle.

War looming

Cardinal Pacelli's high esteem for Montini was evident when the cardinal invited the new surrogate to accompany him when he went to Budapest as papal legate for the

34th International Eucharistic Congress in May 1938. A letter home has a touch of self-mockery. The Vatican delegation was lodged in the Royal Palace and 'it was as though we were all archdukes, or just slightly less, living in a setting of such regal splendour that it seemed almost as though the imperial tradition had never ended'. At dusk there was a marvellous procession of the Host accompanied by boats along the Danube, all fairly lights and hymns and devout, recollected crowds, which continued until long past midnight. But, though an international Catholic event, the Spaniards were absent, engaged in a bitter civil war, and so, too, were the Austrians, annexed and humiliated by Hitler in the *Anschluss* of the same year. Hitler and Mussolini were now firm allies and Pope Pius XI was dying. Montini was the first to be called to the Pope's death-bed at 4am on 10th February 1939 and was present when he was anointed. His future was now problematical and depended on the forthcoming conclave.

Pius XII elected

On 2nd March 1939, after three ballots, followed by a thin trail of white smoke from the chimney of the Sistine Chapel and a clamour of bells, the slight figure of Eugenio Pacelli appeared on the balcony of St Peter's. It was his sixty-third birthday and he took the name Pius XII. The name promised continuity, the election was over in a day, and Montini knew that there would be no question of returning to Brescia as there was still work to be done in Rome. The excitement of the election was captured on film and, in a period of technological advance undreamt of by the protagonists, the event can be relived today on YouTube.

'He was by temperament gentle and rather shy', recalled Tardini of the new pope, 'He wasn't a fighter ... His great goodness led him to wish to please everyone, and to prefer the path of gentleness to that of severity, to persuade rather than to impose.' He quoted an Austrian diplomat who said in 1934 that Pacelli was 'handicapped by a caution that was the result of anxiety, and also by a lack of drive.' These handicaps, perhaps, help to explain Pope Pius XII's ensuing silences during the Second World War. But the Vatican was soon to be placed in a position where it could only keep silence.

Europe was bracing itself for war. Pius's immediate concern after his election was to secure peace. Montini remained in the same office under the new Secretary of State, Cardinal Luigi Maglione, and after Maglioni died in 1944, Montini discharged his duties directly under Pius XII without any intervening Secretary of State. One of Montini's main tasks was liaison with the diplomats accredited to the Vatican but he did not specialise in German affairs and had nothing to do with the negotiations to prevent war. He was the author of the

Pope's 24th August appeal for peace. Tardini and Montini had provided four drafts varying in toughness and the Pope had chosen the least political and most pastoral. Eloquent and moving, the appeal came too late: the die was cast. The next object of Vatican policy was to prevent Italy joining in on the German side but this, too, failed and in 1940 Italy was at war. During the war the Pope entrusted to Montini the organisation and direction of the Holy See's extensive relief work. He was given the responsibility for the Vatican Information Office which brought news of vanished prisoners of war and, where possible, relayed to them messages from their families. Montini helped to hide political refugees, especially Jews, and to help them with means of escape. But he was a reluctant bureaucrat, overwhelmed by work, with too much paper work and too few helpers; he worked on the humblest as well as the highest levels of diplomacy.

Regard for the papacy

During this period of isolation and crisis Montini demonstrated an almost mystical regard for the papal office that transcended temporal affairs. On the evening of 9th February 1941 the Pope took Montini down to the crypt of St Peter's where the tomb of Pius XI had just been completed. Pius lingered and prayed for a long time and also prayed at the tombs of Pius X and Benedict XV. Recalling this event Montini wrote:

> Never had the communion of saints and the spiritual genealogy of the successors of Christ been given, it seemed to me, a more moving expression. And that is very consoling. The Church, this living reality, spiritual and visible, is more present than ever, more modern and necessary than ever; may God who unites and teaches us all be praised.

This experience permanently affected Montini's idea of the papacy. It was an exalted idea of the papal office that some found hard to understand: it placed the pope at the heart of the communion of saints. If anything good were to come out of the tragedy of war, it would be a Church purified and 'more modern and necessary than ever.' He little knew that, in time, he would give this understanding deeper significance and would also be buried nearby.

Vatican surrounded

On 9th September 1943 German troops occupied Rome. There was a serious fear that Pius XII would be arrested and forcibly taken to Germany as a prisoner. This was no idle threat. Goebbels's diary for 26th July 1943 describes Hitler talking with great violence about seizing the Pope and taking over the Vatican. Though the Germans halted at the Vatican frontier when they took Rome, they now had the Vatican at their mercy. 'German troops,' wrote John Conway, the Canadian historian and expert in

German-Jewish relations and the consequences for the Church, 'encircled the tiny Vatican territory on all sides, and a feeling of impotent claustrophobia tinged the panic-filled atmosphere.' The Germans would have arrested the Pope at the first sign of protest and they enjoyed keeping him on tenterhooks.

Personal cost of war

Yet Montini testified that 'Pius XII did what was humanly possible to save human lives and alleviate unspeakable sufferings, even when the swift course of events stifled at birth any chance of success for his charitable activities.' Among many other acts of mercy he saved the lives of 860,000 Jews. Rome was liberated on 4th June 1944. Half a million Romans walked to St Peter's Square with shouts of *Viva il Papa*, and Pius was acclaimed *Defensor Civitatis*. On a personal level, Montini welcomed the liberation because it took pressure off him and he no longer needed to wear a diplomatic mask. During the war not only had his parents died, his parental home in Brescia had been occupied by Germans, his younger brother, Francesco, fought in the Resistance, and his close boyhood friend, Andrea Trebeschi, betrayed by the Fascists, had died in the concentration camp of Guthausen. His elder brother, Lodovico, went on to enter politics and became a senator. Decisive world events became associated with his personal history. The end of the war in Europe virtually coincided with the silver jubilee of Pius XII's episcopal ordination on 29th May 1920, and Montini would die in 1978 on the thirty-third anniversary of the bombing of Hiroshima on 6th August 1945.

Reputation grows

Diplomats considered Msgr Giovanni Battista Montini the most important person in the Vatican after the Pope. He dealt impartially but cordially with the diplomatic representative of all nations. Myron Taylor, Franklin D. Roosevelt's personal representative in the United States State Department considered him 'the most perfect diplomat who achieves his goals quietly and without annoying people'. He further declared that he was 'far and away the most authoritative person in the Vatican, and the most likely candidate to be the next Pope'. This view was partly reached because Montini was responsible for contacts with the outside world, he impressed all whom he met, and, for once, the prophecy would be fulfilled, though later than estimated. Archbishop David Mathew, the English church historian, writer and Apostolic Delegate to the British Colonies, more percipiently conjectured that, because of his key influence, he 'may easily be Pius XIV', Pius being considered a permanent name for the Pope.

But Montini's current task was post-war reconstruction. He intensified the efforts of the

Secretariate of State for the relocation of the homeless. He took a leading part in founding Caritas Internationalis and the Catholic Migration Commission. Constantly interested in social problems, he enthusiastically complied with Pius's orders to foster the establishment of the International Migration Commission.

In 1946 the Christian Democrats, including members that Montini had influenced during his FUCI years, emerged as a political party with a manifesto committed to practical justice and social reform. This was the period that ushered in the Cold War and, in the elections of 1948, the Holy See adopted the Christian Democrat Party, since no other Christian party had any hope of success. Communism posed the most serious threat, filling Pius with pessimism, and he feared the imminent danger to the Church in Italy and the whole of Western Europe. 'If they have a majority,' he asked, 'what can I do to govern the Church as Christ wants Me to govern?' He was offered refuge in Dublin but insisted, 'My place is in Rome and, if it be the will of the Divine Master, I am ready to be martyred for Him in Rome.' The outcome resulted in a Christian Democratic-led coalition gaining 48.5 per cent of the votes, while the United Front of Communists and Socialists had 31 per cent.

Senior role but not a cardinal

During the next nine years Montini practically ran the Secretariat of State in the closing years of Pius's pontificate. He was largely responsible for organising the Holy Year in 1950 and the Marian Year in 1954. In November 1953 he was promoted pro-Secretary of State. These years were difficult as the Pope had become reclusive, fearful and unwell and Montini was one of the few who had relatively easy access to him. 'Why go to the mountain (*monte*),' ran a Roman joke, 'when one can get what one wants from the foothills (*montini*)'. He had enormous influence, a subtle mind informed by wide reading and decisive contacts with intellectuals and theologians, a realistic understanding of the present, and this sometimes led to resentment and suspicion from some of his colleagues. As time passed, it also led to Montini's personal and private reservations about certain papal policies, notably political moves to the right. Due to the rising threat of Communism, at the time it was difficult, almost impossible, to distinguish between politics and theology. The Pope oscillated between Montini and Ottaviani in political questions - Montini a moderate, Ottaviani a hard-line conservative - and this led to Montini's isolation.

Pius XII put the names of Montini and Tardini at the top of a list of new cardinals in 1952. It was confidently expected that Montini would become Secretary of State. Yet when the list of twenty-four cardinals was published prior to the consistory of 1953 neither were included. It has been assumed that in this way the Pope had pointedly excluded

Montini from being a serious candidate as his immediate successor. The reality was that, despite assurances that nothing would change, Montini and Tardini had declined this honour, knowing that the Pope did not intend to appoint a Cardinal Secretary of State. By accepting they would have both lost whatever influence they had; by staying as they were, they still counted; their functions remained unchanged. When Pius fell gravely ill in January 1954, he saw no one except his doctors, Montini and Tardini.

The French, *resourcement* and liturgy

From his years as a young priest Montini had, through reading, been Francophile in his sympathies. Through the Apostolic Nuncio to France, Bishop Angelo Roncalli (later Pope John XXIII), he became interested in such movements as the *Renouveau Catholique* and later in the *Mission de France*, and Montini enthusiastically supported the priest-workers, despite the suspicion and hostility with which many of his colleagues in the Roman Curia viewed the experiment. The Church in France after the war was marked by a theological and social renewal which faced contemporary challenges. The Dominicans, Yves Congar and Marie-Dominique Chenu, and the Jesuit, Henry de Lubac, spearheaded the theological principle of *resourcement* (return to the sources) a retrieval and renewal of Catholic thought which came to be known as *la nouvelle théologie*. The Dominican Jacques Loew, the priest-docker from Marseilles, actively promoted the priest-worker movement. This was concerned with relevance to the world of work and some priest-workers misunderstood the spirit of Christianity and put themselves on the same level as Marxists. These moves coincided with the intensified Marxist persecution of the Church throughout Eastern Europe and the situation became graver with the imprisonment of Cardinal Stefan Wyszynski, Primate of Poland, in September 1953. The priest-workers were suppressed in the same year and severe measures were taken against the Dominicans, narrowly avoiding their suppression. The progressive wing of the French Church was mortally struck by the blow.

Montini recognised the implications of the threat, especially as far as it concerned the priest-workers, but he helped organise a mediating mission which was sent to Paris to assure the French bishops that the Holy See had not lost confidence in them and would arrange a new statute for the priest-workers. Montini's role was to soften the blows, not to avert them. Yet in the Vatican he was seen to be pro-French and the French believed that he understood them better than others in Rome. Influential colleagues came to regard him as dangerous and began to plot his downfall.

Victim of intrigue

This came to a head when he contributed a preface, written in French, to a two-volume collection of the papal texts on the priesthood from Pius X to Pius XII, edited by Msgr Pierre Veuillot, a French colleague in the Secretary of State, published in 1954. The book was regarded as a conformist endorsement of the papal position as far as it concerned the priest-workers. But writing for a French audience, Montini had in mind French models. He began by saying that the synthesis not only threw light on the priesthood but also on the Church. It is in the priest that the nature of the Church appears 'in its institutional features, its specific functions, and its perpetual effort to sanctify the world'. This did not immediately emerge from the text but was the fruit of his personal reflection and prayer.

The liturgical movement had focused on the essential role of the priest as the celebrant of the Mass:

> Some have admirably devoted themselves to revivifying the liturgy from within, giving meaning and poetry to the prayers we use; the rites appear in their authentic austerity and beauty; the celebration of the mystery reawakens the sense of the ineffable union of divine and human in the sacramental action; a tremor of mysterious joy, of divine presence and human charity ripples through the group praying round the altar; the priest is filled with joy; the springtime of the Church blossoms.

This reflected Montini's own Masses celebrated for FUCI on the principles found in Romano Guardini and Pius Parsch, the Austrian Augustinian liturgist of Klosterneuburg

- 'You shouldn't pray at Mass, you should pray the Mass'. But he went on to define the role of the priest as evangelist rather than minister to an élite group.

> There is no point in ringing your bell if no one is listening to it. The priest has to listen to the sirens from the factories, these temples of technology where the modern world vibrates. It's up to the priest to become a missionary, if he wants Christianity to remain and become the living leaven of civilisation.

'Priesthood is a social service,' he concluded, 'the priest is a man for others. Priesthood and egoism exclude each other; priesthood and charity coincide.' A priest was one who should 'get drunk on God' (*s'enivrer de Dieu*). Montini was drawing from his own experience rather than restating the grounds of the priest-worker movement. For him pastoral work was an art rather than a science. But the preface did little to disabuse some of his Vatican colleagues in their view of him as a dangerous man.

Archbishop of Milan

On 29th August 1954 Cardinal Ildefonso Schuster OSB, Archbishop of Milan, died aged seventy-three, leaving vacant the most prestigious see of Italy; it was one of the largest jurisdictions in the world. Pressure was put on the Pope to appoint Montini to the diocese and the announcement was made on 3rd December. After thirty-four years in Rome Montini was presented as Pius XII's 'personal gift' to Milan and on 12th December, *Gaudete* Sunday, he was ordained bishop in St Peter's Basilica by Cardinal Eugène Tisserant and the Milanese present, recognising his prestige, applauded him out of the basilica. Vladimir d'Ormeson, the French Ambassador, said that 'what we have most respected and loved in you is that behind the diplomatic official, we have always found a priest'. And in his dispatches to the Quai d'Orsay he bluntly blamed Montini's departure on 'the reactionary gang (*clan*) which had more and more influence over Pius XII as he grew older, weaker, more and more obsessed by Communism'. They had achieved their shoddy aim of removing him from Rome and prevented him from becoming a cardinal for as long as possible.

New role as archbishop

Filled with private anxiety, Archbishop Montini left Rome for Milan on 4th January 1955 (with two removal vans containing the 8000 books of his library) to assume the pastoral care of a diocese with 1000 churches, 2500 priests and 3,500,000 souls. In a letter to Giulio Bavilacquau he wrote of the days of intense suffering he had experienced when he contemplated the immensity of the task before him:

> What will happen? I can see a tangle of problems, a host of difficulties enough to make me dizzy; and once again I am assailed by the temptation of faint-heartedness. But from now on I will have to give a real and positive assent to divine help. Continue to pray for me. Please share with me whatsoever ideas your experience and affection suggest.

He was to remain there for eight years until his election to the Apostolic See in 1963. During his period in Milan, Montini was known as one of the most progressive members of the Catholic hierarchy and, while ill-at-ease in the presence of simple people, a friend of the working class; this made further enemies among the right and attracted ridicule, but was in tune with his development. When he arrived the city offered a microcosm of Italy. It was poised for the great leap forward dubbed an 'economic miracle'; it was rapidly becoming industrialised and attracted thousands of migrants from the impoverished regions of Southern Italy.

Montini knew that a potentially divided city would result - rich in the centre, poor in the new suburbs - and he urged in a letter to a suburban priest, 'Milan must love Milan, ancient Milan must love modern Milan.' He worked strenuously to unite the old with the new. He preached a message of love 'to the unfortunates who gather behind Marx', and assured the workers that 'Jesus still loves you strongly, divinely, immensely'. He encouraged a new priestly association called the Missionaries of the World of Work - the best he could do after the banning of the French priest-workers; they were known as 'the Archbishop's left-wingers'. In 1956, the first anniversary of his arrival was marked in retaliation by a right-wing bomb being thrown through the window of his residence but caused little damage; the last Archbishop of Milan who was subjected to an attempted assassination was St Charles Borromeo.

Daring initiatives

Montini wanted the worship in the cathedral to be a model for the whole diocese. Milan had its own Ambrosian rite - the only diocese in the West, bar Toledo, that had this privilege. Many of Milan's churches had been bombed in August 1943 and he became a great builder of churches, increasing the number by more than ten per cent, with forty-one in Milan itself and seventy-four scattered in the diocese. 'Wherever a church is,' he wrote, 'it becomes a centre; it is not an encumbrance; it is the pivot of communication; a place where you can look out on modest houses or vast skyscrapers and get a comforting, ordering, inspiring perspective.' He believed that the Milanese should be taught how to pray well and re-opened chapels in abandoned convents and monasteries. He created new parishes and subdivided old ones, and he made pastoral visitations to 694 parishes. Montini did not simply build churches; he also constructed schools, community centres and dispensaries in the poor districts of Milan. Through the already existing Domus Ambrosiana he had an entire village constructed at Rovagnasco to provide housing for 3000 poor people. In addition, he established an Office of Charity to provide free medical and legal advice, and he often visited orphanages, hospitals, nursing homes for the aged, prisons, and reformatories. Through his work for the poor he became known as 'the priest of the left', a title he detested; he preferred to be known as the 'archbishop of the workers'. The champion of all who were oppressed, he believed that this did not commit him to any particular political ideology. Though Montini's natural world was with the educated middle class, he preached the social message of the Gospel, and strove unceasingly in the Communist stronghold of Milan to win the labouring class back to the Church.

In November 1957 Montini held the Mission to Milan, aimed mainly at lapsed Catholics, and conducted for three weeks in all the parishes of the city, in institutions, schools, cinemas, factories and on the street-corners. 'People of Milan,' declared the posters, 'from 10th to 24th November a thousand voices will speak to you of God.' More than five hundred priests, twenty-four bishops, two cardinals and countless lay collaborators delivered more than 7000 sermons. The priests were called the 'flying friars' because they were equipped with small motorbikes and Montini himself sped around the diocese in the fastest car he could find, a passion he continued in Rome. *Paris-Match* described it as 'the monster-mission'; Cardinal Sergio Pignedoli, then Auxiliary Bishop of Milan, who visited seventy-one places during its course, later boasted that 'it was the greatest experiment of its kind in the history of the Catholic Church'. Montini's friend, Jean Guitton, reported that 1283 sites were used to deliver the message, and that the 'strategy was to give the city a functional shock, as a Protestant mission had done in the City of New York, to shake up atheistic indifference'.

Pope John XXIII makes him Cardinal

On 9th October 1958 at 3.52am Pope Pius XII died at Castelgandolfo. He was succeeded by Angelo Guiseppe Roncalli, Patriarch of Venice, and took the name of John.

Pope John XXIII's election changed Montini's life. On 17th November the world learned that he would be Pope John's first cardinal. Then, on 25th January 1959, John announced the calling of an Ecumenical Council of the Roman Catholic Church.

The Second Vatican Council

Renewing the life of the Church

It was widely held that the decision to convene the Second Vatican Council was apparently due to a sudden inspiration of the Holy Spirit. The background to making this decision was more complex. On the night before his election to the Papacy two conservative cardinals, Ernesto Ruffini, Archbishop of Palermo, and Alfred Ottaviani, secretary to the Holy Office, suggested to Roncalli, the successful candidate, that there should be a general council. In 1948 they had first proposed a council to Pius XII for four reasons. They believed that doctrinal errors were inflicting harm on the faithful; that canon law needed to be brought up to date (they coined the term *aggiornamento*); Catholics had to be united against Communism; and it could be an occasion for the definition of the dogma of the Assumption of Mary. Pius XII did not choose a conciliar route to address these questions because it was a common view in the Church that, after the definition of papal primacy and infallibility at the Vatican Council of 1869-70, councils were unnecessary. But he made tentative moves in this direction, and handed the planning over to Cardinal Ottaviani's Holy Office.

From this unexpected source John at the age of seventy-six took the risk of convening the Council. If Montini had been appointed Pius XII's successor as some wanted, though he was not then a cardinal, it is unlikely that this would have happened. The Church at that date appeared so well structured and secure that it seemed better to let well alone. John defined the Council's immediate task as renewing the life of the Church and bringing up to date its teaching, discipline and organisation, with the unity of all Christians as the ultimate goal. This was an agenda subtly different from the original proposals but the Holy Office believed that they were firmly in place. On the evening of the day the Council was announced, Montini telephoned his old Brescian Oratorian friend, Giulio Bevilacqua, with the news and said, 'This holy old boy doesn't realise what a hornet's nest he is stirring up.' Bevilacqua told him not to worry but trust the Holy Spirit 'still awake and about in the Church'.

Next day Montini published a hopeful message to the diocese.

> The Council will be the greatest that the Church has ever celebrated in the twenty centuries of its history, the greatest in numbers and in spiritual impact, called in complete and peaceful unity with the hierarchy. It will be the most 'catholic' in its dimensions, truly reaching to the whole world and all civil societies.

John's convocation of the 21st Ecumenical Council of the Universal Church, known as the Second Vatican

Council, launched the most radical change of direction for the Catholic Church since the Council of Trent, held from 1545-63. Vatican II, whose four sessions lasted from October 1962 to December 1965, has been labelled 'the end of the Counter-Reformation'. Forty-three years later it is still too soon to establish a clear sense of perspective about the Council's aims and achievements. It was not what John intended (he expected it to last for no longer than two months) and its continuity and application was entirely due to Montini after his election as Pope in 1963. An overview of its progress is necessary in order to assess the significance of Pope Paul VI's involvement.

Few bishops who entered St Peter's at the opening had any idea of what would follow. The interior was transformed by hangings of red silk, raked stalls extended for the entire length, boxes for observers were positioned in the midst of the arcades, the assembled bishops wore classic Roman copes, John sat on the gilded throne of Pope Leo XIII in front of the high altar, the arrangements were the same as those for the First Vatican Council. But the members of the Council were assisted by several thousand experts (*periti*) in theology, canon law and church history. There were also present in an unofficial capacity (though without the right to speak or vote) observers from the main denominations not in communion with the Catholic Church.

The sessions

The Council consisted of four sessions but though the first issued a 'Message to Humanity' on 20th October, when it adjourned in December it had made no formal decisions. On the second day the assembled prelates took a recess to elect their own committee members and thus indicated their independence of the Roman Curia. Soon after, Montini himself had been elected Pope. The second session (September-November 1964) showed support for the collegiality of bishops, the divine right of the episcopal college, and the restitution of the diaconate as a separate and permanent order. After the close of the session the Council promulgated a Constitution on the Sacred Liturgy and a decree on the Instruments of Social Communication. The third session (September-November 1964) promulgated the Dogmatic Constitution on the Church, the Decree on Ecumenism, and the Decree on the Eastern Catholic Churches; and Paul proclaimed the Blessed Virgin Mary to be the Mother of the Church.

The documents

The fourth, and most extensive, session (September-December 1965) concluded the Council. In an Apostolic Constitution on 15th September the Pope formulated the norms for the new episcopal synod which was to be established to assist him to govern the Church. On 28th

September the following documents were promulgated: the Decree on the Bishops' Pastoral Office in the Church, the Decree on the Appropriate Renewal of the Religious Life, the Decree on Priestly Formation, the Declaration on Christian Education, the Declaration on the Relationship of the Church to Non-Christian Religions. To these were added on 18 November the Dogmatic Constitution on Divine Revelation and the decree on the Apostolate of the Laity. Paul also announced the beginning of the reform of the Roman Curia and the introduction of the process of beatification of Pius XII and John XXIII. On 4th December a Service of Prayer (*Sacra Celebratio*) for Promoting Christian Unity took place at St Paul's-Without-the-Walls. In this the delegated observers and guests took part. On 7th December were promulgated a Declaration on Religious Freedom, the Decree on the Ministry and Life of Priests, the Decree on the Church's Missionary Activity, and the Pastoral Constitution on the Church in the Modern World. Most of the decrees have had a considerable influence on the life of the Catholic Church ever since. The next day the Council was solemnly closed. It had assumed spiritual and historical dimensions of incalculable significance.

Early reservations

Montini was frequently consulted by John, and was influential in the early preparations for the Council (he sat on the Central Preparatory Commission and the Technical-Organisational Commission); he was active in the opening stages but his attitude to the first session, at which he spoke only twice, was cool, not to say critical. He was appointed a member of the Secretariat convened to examine the questions raised by members of the Council. The first session fell into organisational chaos under the weight of its documents. It was Cardinal Leo-Joseph Suenens, Archbishop of Mechelin-Brussel, the primatial Belgian see, who, at the invitation of the Pope, rescued it from deadlock and essentially set the agenda for the whole Council. All present knew that John clearly could not be expected to last indefinitely and a new pope would soon be needed. This, perhaps, explains his silence and restraint. Cardinal Suenens noted that Montini 'remained reserved during the Council'. But he published weekly articles on the Council in *L'Italia*, the Milanese Catholic daily newspaper, stressing the point of liturgical change, under the heading 'From the Vatican'. His first intervention defended change in order that the prayer of the Church might be pastorally more effective and steered a middle course between 'arbitrary liturgical innovations' and doing nothing.

On 12th November 1962 it was announced that there would be a second and concluding session in 1963, from 12th May to 29th June, but on the night of 25th-26th November, on his eighty-first birthday, John had a serious haemorrhage. This presaged the end of his life. On 31st May, four days before his death, Montini and the Pope's brothers, Zaverio, Alfredo and Guiseppe, and his surviving sister Assunta, were summoned to his deathbed and prayed until late into the night. On 3rd June at 7.49am, John died, after reigning for less than five years - the shortest pontificate of the century until the reign of Pope John Paul I, lasting for a month in 1978.

Steering the Church in troubled times

At the conclave held between 17th-21st June following the Pope's death, attended by eighty cardinals, and the largest so far in history, Giovanni Battista Montini was elected as John's successor at the sixth ballot. He was sixty-five and his choice of the name, Paul, suggested an outward-looking approach. In his radio message on the day following the election, Pope Paul recalled his three immediate predecessors who, he said, 'have left us a sacred and glorious spiritual heritage: Pius XI, with his indomitable strength of mind; Pius XII, who illuminated the Church with the light of a teaching full of wisdom; John XXIII, who gave to the entire world an example of singular goodness'. Privately, Paul wrote about his feelings in a note written on the day of the election:

> Perhaps the Lord has called me to this service not because I have any aptitude for it, not so much that I can govern the Church in its present difficulties, but so that I may suffer something and thus that it may be clear that it is the Lord, and no one else, who guides and saves it.

Montini as pope

Paul would come to suffer deeply in his pontificate, but at the outset his actions were marked by an immense, serene, and confident vigour. Greatly under the spell of his predecessor, he immediately promised to continue the Second Vatican Council; and announced that he would also revise canon law, promote justice in civil, social and international life, and work for peace and the unity of Christendom. He declared that his entire pontificate would be devoted to the Council and its consequences. Even before the coronation (Paul was the last pope to be crowned with the triple tiara) he had already established the date for reopening the Council.

Paul took the Council over and gave it direction by clarifying its goals: the renewal of the Church, the promotion of Christian unity, and dialogue with the modern world. Before the opening of the sessions he had issued a revised *Ordo Concilii* to expedite business, and he introduced a number of procedural reforms, such as the admission of laymen as auditors and the establishment of a press committee. In November 1963 he enlarged the Concilear Commissions to make them more representative. Before the meeting of the Third Session in 1964 he also admitted women, both religious and lay, as auditors. He refused to intervene in the Third Session when he was asked to overrule a decision postponing a vote on the schema on religious liberty, but on his own authority he modified the Decree on Ecumenism and he declared the Blessed Virgin Mary Mother of the Church, despite the fact that the fathers of the Council had refused to attribute the title to her. He also directed that an explanatory note (*nota praevia*) be added to the text of the 1964 Dogmatic Constitution on the Church containing important clarifications on collegiality which elucidated its emphasis on episcopal authority at the alleged expense of papal authority. At the Fourth Session he announced that he was establishing a permanent Synod of Bishops, which would have deliberative as well as consultative powers at the Pope's discretion. His hesitation on documents concerning religious liberty, ecumenism, and the Jews were all motivated by a desire to ensure that the defeated minority of opponents were not simply crushed; he wanted them to be convinced, not vanquished (*convaincus pas vaincus*).

Some have seen Paul as a man caught between two worlds. Nearly all his experience of church government had been acquired under Pius XII, either as a member of Cardinal Pacelli's department when the future Pope was Secretary of State, or running the Secretariat himself during the final years of Pius's pontificate. For the first few months, Paul tried to follow not only the policies, but also the style, of John. But he shared Pius's exalted vision of the papal office and he eventually came to model himself upon him rather than John. The tension between these two styles was to plague him throughout his pontificate and some have regretted that he chose the Pian model. In retrospect, the combination of both was his principal strength.

Turmoil in Church and world

Torn between a confident forward-looking vision and his suspicion of any innovation which might undermine the integrity and authority of the Church's teaching, he consistently emphasised the mystery and other-worldliness of the faith, and dreaded anything suggestive of scientific naturalism. John had described him as 'a little like Hamlet' because of his ambiguity and apparent indecisiveness but Paul himself repudiated this definition. It was these two apparently contradictory factors which enabled him to steer the Church through a period of radical change and keep it together without major schism in the troubled years immediately following the Council. At the start of the Council Paul wrote optimistically that 'a highly civilised and advanced world is engaged in search, marked by suffering, but journeying unwittingly towards Christ.' Few, if any, of the Council fathers expected the social, moral and political turmoil of the years from 1965-70 and their effects on the implementation of the Council's decrees. Fewer still would have anticipated the evolution of a secularised, post-Christian society.

'Rarely did a pontificate begin is such discouraging circumstances,' wrote an anonymous commentator, 'Never did the keys of St Peter seem so heavy.' One of the main problems was an international misunderstanding of the character of Pope John XXIII. His kind-heartedness and goodness raised impossible expectations and misunderstandings. 'Serious harm is done to the memory of Pope John', Paul wrote, 'when people assign him attitudes that were not his.' John believed in traditional doctrine and practice and Paul told Jean Guitton, 'Pope John was much more conservative than me, much more traditional.' He knew that he could never fulfil the expectations aroused by this mythical view of good Pope John. One of his first actions was to have the papal apartments cleared of the red silk and gilding of his predecessors, hang the walls with grey velvet (a fashion then popular in Milan) and simplify the furniture. This was perceived as a modernising tendency that anticipated much that was to come and symbolised the austerity of post-conciliar reform. Paul's aesthetic remains in the papal apartments to this day.

Journey to the Holy Land

Paul was the first reigning pontiff ever to have ridden in an aeroplane and helicopter and the first modern pope to have travelled to the Near East. On 4th-6th January 1964 he made an unprecedented pilgrimage to the Holy Land with the twofold intention of emphasising the point that ecclesiology was founded on the rock of St Peter's faith and in order to meet Athenagorus II, the Ecumenical Patriarch of Constantinople. The pilgrimage to the Holy

Land gave an evangelical and ecumenical direction to his pontificate. These meetings led to the historic gesture of friendship with the Eastern Orthodox Church: before Mass on 7th December 1965 a joint declaration was read in which Paul and Anthenagorus expressed their mutual regret for the events of 1054, when Cardinal Humbert of Silva Candida and Patriarch Michael Cerularius had excommunicated each other and created the Great Schism between the Western and Eastern Church. A Roman Catholic Pontiff had not met officially with an Orthodox Patriarch since 1439. After the Mass the Pope exchanged embraces with Athenagorus's envoy; thus indicating that they belonged to 'sister churches'. Further ecumenical relations were established after the establishment of the permanent secretariat for the Promotion of Christian Unity. He received in Rome on 24th March 1966 the Archbishop of Canterbury, Michael Ramsey, visited Athenagorus again in Istanbul on 25th July 1967 and received him in Rome on 26th October in the same year. Archbishop Ramsey's visit was followed by the establishment of the joint Anglican-Roman Catholic International Commission (ARCIC) in 1968.

First encyclical and foreign journeys

Paul's early journeys had an influence on the Council because, apart from their intrinsic significance, they spoke of the Church's relations with non-Christian religions and with non-believers - the outer fringe of humanity he spoke of in his first encyclical, *Ecclesiam Suam*, in 1964. His second visit that year was to India, a land of ancient Christian traditions that welcomed him as a holy man. He then went to the United Nations in New York on the Feast of St Francis, 4th October 1965, met the whole world in microcosm and made a fervent plea for peace before the General Assembly of the United Nations. His praise for the work of the United Nations was well received and he was hailed by millions in a day that ended with a pontifical Mass at the Yankee Stadium. In 1966 he longed to go to Poland for the millennium celebrations but the Polish Communist government denied his request. In 1967 he visited Portugal to commemorate the fiftieth anniversary of the apparition at Fatima and addressed a huge crowd of two million. In late August 1968 he went to Columbia, to attend the Eucharistic Congress at Bogotà and the Latin American Episcopal Conference (CELAM) at Medellin. He addressed the World Council of Churches and the International Labour Organisation in Geneva in 1969, visited Uganda to honour the martyrs in the same year, and the Philippines (where an unsuccessful attempt was made on his life by a madman disguised as a priest) and Australia in 1970. For the first time in history Peter in the person of Paul established an apostolic contact with the world and anticipated the universal travel of Pope John

Paul II. The Pope was no longer the 'prisoner of the Vatican' but belonged to all people.

The fourth and final period of the Second Vatican Council began on 14th September 1965, the feast of the Exaltation of the Holy Cross, and ended on 8th December, the feast of the Immaculate Conception. In three years a marked change had come over the proceedings. Gone was the panoply of papal Rome. Paul entered St Peter's on foot instead of on the *sedia gestatoria*, wearing a simple cope instead of the heavy papal mantum, a mitre rather than the tiara, and carried a pastoral staff of silver he had designed himself, made by the sculptor Lello Scorzelli, representing Christ hanging on the cross. He joined the collegial ranks of the bishops, and enthroned the book of the Gospels himself as a symbol of his primacy. The ecumenical service in St Paul-Without-the-Walls was equally simple. Paul sat on a strait-backed chair on ground level and read from a flimsy pamphlet rather than a buckram-bound volume embossed with the papal arms. Readers represented the three main Christian traditions: Catholic, Orthodox and Protestant: The Council concluded with messages to rulers, intellectuals, women, the sick and suffering, workers and young people delivered in St Peter's Square. These innovations anticipated the Council's aftermath. Paul proclaimed an extraordinary Jubilee or Holy Year, to be observed from

1st January to Pentecost (29th May) 1966, in order that the faithful might be familiarised with the teaching of the Council and the life of the Church renewed.

He established a number of post-conciliar Commissions to put into effect the wishes of the Council. The most far-reaching reforms of his pontificate were effected largely through the workings of these Commissions. Other reforms, such as that of the *Codex Juris Canonici*, the Church's Canon Law, were put in hand, though this was completed under Pope John Paul II. Paul's encyclicals were more conservative; the most important include *Mysterium Fidei*, promulgated on 3rd September 1965, which reaffirmed the traditional doctrine of the Eucharist. *Popularum Progressio*, promulgated on 16th March 1967, dealt with social, economic and political issues, the duty of aiding developing nations, and committed the Church to working for justice throughout the whole world. Where Pius XII had spoken to the conscience of Catholics, Paul addressed the conscience of all mankind. *Sacerdotalis coelibitus*, promulgated on 24th June 1967, insisted on the need for priestly celibacy. *Humanae Vitae*, promulgated on 25th July 1968, condemned all artificial methods of birth control for Catholics except the rhythm method, created a crisis and attracted widespread criticism. In many ways it was the watershed of Paul's papacy and caused serious repercussions.

Humanae vitae and birth control

The Christian principles determining the ethics of contraception, procreation and abortion are associated with the sacredness of human life, love of neighbour, and respect for the sovereignty and providence of God. On the basis of these principles early Christian thinkers, in contrast to their pagan contemporaries, were united in their condemnation of infanticide and abortion. Abortion was forbidden at the Council of Elvira c306. The general teaching of the Fathers against contraception was related to this set of attitudes and was shaped by an insistence on the integrity of the Old Testament teaching that procreation within marriage was good, combined with reasoning which asserted the unnaturalness of a sexual act which did not have procreation as its end.

These early prohibitions predominated in Christian teaching until recent times when there was questioning about traditional attitudes to contraception and abortion. In 1930 Pius XI affirmed traditional teaching in the encyclical, *Casti Conubii*, which condemned any use of marriage 'in the exercise of which the act, by human effort, is deprived of its natural power of procreating life.' This document in passing acknowledged the legitimacy of intercourse during the infertile period, the rhythm method, later positively accepted by Pius XII in 1951. Alternatively, the Lambeth Conference of 1930 declared that there is 'a clearly felt moral obligation to limit or avoid parenthood, and where there is a morally sound reason for avoiding complete abstinence...other methods may be used' (Resolution 115). This qualified acceptance in the Anglican Communion of the propriety of artificial contraception was a sign of the change of view on this topic which has prevailed in the mainstream Protestant denominations ever since. At that time contraception was effected by barrier methods.

The pill

Funded by Margaret Sanger, an American campaigner for women's rights, Carl Djerassi first invented the human contraceptive pill at a laboratory in Mexico in 1951. She coined the phrase 'birth control' and raised $150,000 to accomplish this end. Frank Colton, an American chemist, developed the first commercially available oral contraceptive named Enovid in 1960, produced by G. G. Searle & Co. It was a combination of synthetic hormones, oestragen and protestogen, taken to prevent conception by hampering the monthly release of an egg cell from the ovary. In 1964 Searle took $24m in net profits from sales of the pill. In 1961, despite reservations from doctors about the long-term effects on health, women in Britain were able to get oral contraception on the National Health Service and the use of the pill spread throughout the western world. Not only did the pill prevent human conception, for the first time in history it placed women on an equal basis with men as far as sexual relations were concerned and changed the essential purpose of sex as the primary force that creates human life. This led to profound, far-ranging social consequences that had a universal effect.

A Papal Commission was appointed by Pope John in 1963 and confirmed by Paul on his election to look into the moral and ethical implications of this new method. The majority of the Commission appears to have favoured the legitimacy of contraception in certain circumstances. Paul's Catholic critics insisted that they were talking about the responsible use of contraception within a stable marriage to space births where children already existed. The encyclical takes its stand on the sanctity of Natural Law, condemns abortion, sterilisation, or any action which, in connection with the conjugal act, intends 'to render procreation impossible'. But it also emphasises the importance of human love and calls for responsible parenthood. Natural Law shows the inseparable connection, willed by God and unable to be broken by human beings on their own initiative, between the unitive and the procreative meaning of the sexual act. Natural family planning is acceptable because it makes a legitimate use of a natural disposition and does not impede the development of natural processes. The grave social consequences of artificial birth control are identified and encouragement is given to those who find the teaching difficult and the effort required by individuals, families and society at large.

Rationale and consequences

Paul saw *Humanae Vitae* as a prophetic document and many would argue that subsequent history has proved him right. The morality of contraception involved absolutes on which he could not yield. The key lay in the perennial debate about the ends or goals of marriage. Once the unitive meaning of sexual intercourse was separated from its procreative meaning, there was no case to be made against any kind of sexual gratification. Paul's Catholic opponents pointed to an ideal of marriage in which limited contraception might be permissible. But there was no known way of limiting contraception to such admirable families. Inevitably, there would be other, less responsible users of birth control who simply saw it as a way of having sex without having children.

Humanae Vitae immediately raised a storm of protest. Its teaching was specifically repudiated by the 1968 Lambeth Conference. He expected to be criticised and misunderstood by the secular media and those in the Church suffering from anti-Roman prejudice but he also expected absolute loyalty from the cardinals and bishops. Hence his pain when this manifestly did not happen. The papal diplomatic corps was ordered by the Secretary of

State to produce evidence of spontaneous adhesion of groups or prominent individuals. *L'Orservatore Romano* excelled itself, printing these and other instances of enthusiastic support from all over the world and never once admitted that there was a breath of criticism. But it soon became evident that the encyclical did not enjoy the wholehearted support of all the bishops. In a spirit of collegiality with and under the Pope, Paul had promoted local groups of bishops to meet in episcopal conferences to deal with problems in their geographical areas. He established a series of regular meetings in Rome for bishops' representatives to discuss more general questions. But, as was his right, some questions he reserved to himself, and refused to submit to collegial decisions. One was the celibacy of the clergy, the other was *Humanae Vitae*. They had not expected the Pope to act unilaterally, without consultation, as the Supreme Pontiff. Unhappily the encyclical was ignored by many Catholics, and treated warily by many of the clergy.

While Paul remained confident of the rightness of his decision, he was profoundly shaken by the critical international reaction to it. It was a turning point in his pontificate. He published no more encyclicals, though of course other documents flowed from his pen, and later said to a Vatican diplomat, 'Now I understand St Peter: he came to Rome twice, the second time to be crucified.' The controversy dragged on throughout his reign, and overshadowed it. One result led to the hardening of doctrinal positions in the Church, orthodox and conservative, liberal and progressive, which still remain.

The consequences of the mass use of the pill and the legalisation of abortion, resulting not only in widespread hedonism but depopulation and the undermining of the family, lie all around. Some western governments are now offering financial incentives to married people to have children. This encyclical, in company with *Populorum Progressio*, was the glory of Paul's pontificate. Its teaching formed the basis of Pope John Paul II's four-year catechesis on the theology of the body in 1979-84, and the teaching was reiterated by him in the encyclical, *Evangelium Vitae*, in 1995 In 2008 Pope Benedict XVI addressed the participants of the Congress on the fortieth anniversary of *Humanae Vitae* and said: 'The truth in *Humanae Vitae* does not change; rather, in the light of the new scientific findings, its teaching becomes even more up-to-date and induces reflection upon its intrinsic value.'

New Missal, Lectionary and Breviary

The most notable reform of Paul's pontificate was the publication of a new Roman Missal in 1970 with an accompanying lectionary and the new breviary in 1971, which together involved a reordering of the Mass and Office. Later, consideration was given to the possibility of adapting liturgies for use in different parts of the world where different cultures prevail. This was the most important decision of his pontificate, more important even than *Humanae Vitae*, because it profoundly affected the spiritual lives of Catholics universally, their imaging of God and worship. The liturgical developments in the Catholic Church also profoundly affected non-Catholic denominations and transformed worship far beyond the boundaries of the Roman Catholic Church.

On 4th December 1963, the Council had issued a Constitution on the Sacred Liturgy known as *Sacrosanctum Concilium*. Section 50 read as follows:

> The rite of the Mass is to be revised in such a way that the intrinsic nature and purpose of its several parts, as also the connection between them, may be more clearly manifested, and that devout and active participation by the faithful may be more easily achieved.
>
> For this purpose the rites are to be simplified, due care being taken to preserve their substance; elements which, with the passage of time, came to be duplicated, or were added with but little advantage, are now to be discarded; other elements which have suffered injury through accidents of history are now to be restored to the vigour which they had in the days of the holy Fathers, as may seem useful or necessary.

Sacrosanctum Concilium further provided that a greater use of the Scriptures should be made at Mass and that, while the use of Latin was to be preserved in the Latin rite, the vernacular languages should be more widely employed. The crucial influence on adopting the vernacular came from bishops in Communist countries. Under the Communist system, formal preaching and teaching about religion was forbidden and Mass in the vernacular, communicated by the words of the rite, was the only way of disseminating scripture, doctrine and the truths of the Faith.

Paul and the liturgical movement

The decree was the fruit of the liturgical movement which had received its chief impetus from the directions of Pope Pius X in 1903 in the promotion of Eucharistic piety and frequent Communion. It was especially fostered by the Benedictines in France, Belgium and Germany. From c1910 the movement spread to the Netherlands, Italy and England and later to the United States of America and elsewhere. After the Second World War, in France and Germany the momentum of the movement advanced outside the monastic centres into the parochial and missionary spheres, and from then on it took a more pastoral direction. In his encyclical *Mediator Dei* (1947) Pius XII gave considerable encouragement to the liturgical movement by his insistence on the importance of the liturgy and the need for the participation of the people, though at the same time he stressed the need for proper order. From this time permission was given for the use of the vernacular in the administration of all sacraments except the Mass; and the reform of the rites began with the revision of the Holy Week liturgy in 1951 and 1955. The Council endorsed the aims of the liturgical movement and gave them general application.

From 1963 modifications were made to the existing Roman Rite but the new Missal quickly exerted a profound change in Catholic worship. Long centuries of liturgical immobility had given an exaggerated conception of changelessness and few were prepared for the *Novus Ordo*. To Jean Guitton Paul defended the Missal in the name of tradition: 'Not only have we maintained everything of the past but we have rediscovered the most ancient and primitive tradition, the one closest to the origins. This tradition has been obscured in the course of centuries, particularly by the Council of Trent.' The reforms were not only intended as a return to primitive simplicity and Eucharistic authenticity, but also as a reflection of the simplicity of Christ. These views surprised all but the liturgically educated and their followers. They led to a greater clarity of expression in an attempt to make worship more corporate and intelligible. The Constitution on the Sacred Liturgy was published on 4th December 1963.

Between 1964-70 Latin was virtually abandoned, Mass was said facing the people in hastily adapted sanctuaries, ceremonies and vestments were simplified; worship became more congregational, and popularist music replaced Gregorian chant, polyphony and the classical repertoire. Yet, despite the drastic external cost, the reforms won their way and now represent the ordinary pattern of Catholic worship.

'The smoke of Satan'

Liturgically and historically sound though the Missal was and apt in its pastoral application, spontaneous informality entered worship, beauty was abandoned, and this led to one of Paul's most enigmatic utterances in which he declared that 'through some crack in the temple of God, the smoke of Satan has entered'. What did he mean by this disturbing statement and was it accurately reported? Many believed that they referred to dissent from the authentic voice of the Church's *Magisterium* and the emergence of polarised doctrinal positions; the sermon in which it occurred was recorded in *L'Osservatore Romano*. Cardinal Virgilio Noe (Paul's master of ceremonies and one who welcomed the reforms) explained in an interview in 2008 that what the Pope meant 'referred to those priests who turned Holy Mass into straw in the name of creativity, but who in truth were possessed of the vainglory and the pride of the Evil

One. Therefore, the smoke of Satan was none other than the mentality that wanted to distort the traditional canons and liturgy of the Eucharistic ceremony.' Hard words, but they emphasise Paul's orthodox integrity in promulgating the Missal; he was not prepared for maimed rites.

Liturgical chaos and iconoclasm were, with notable exceptions, symptomatic of the general tumult that swept the world as a result of the left-wing student uprising of 1968 (which included many young Catholics), international terrorism, the Vietnam War, the permissive society and the emergence of global capitalism. Socially these phenomena, helped by post-modernist types of philosophy taught in the universities, did more to challenge the application of the Council in the immediate aftermath than any other influences. All authority figures were called into question. The dawn of an age of dissent marked the life of entire generations; no climate could have been more difficult for the implementation of the Council. It was left to the future to apply the fruits of Vatican II authentically.

The Creed of the people of God

In 1967 Paul called a Year of Faith to celebrate the apostles Peter and Paul on the occasion of the nineteenth centenary of their martyrdom. It was concluded on 3rd June 1968 with the proclamation of a solemn profession of faith called 'The Creed of the People of God' which retraced the formulas of the Nicene Creed. On the Feast of Christ the King that same year it was recited in many churches throughout the world. This was written by his old friend Jacques Maritain and answered doubts cast by the controversial *Dutch Catechism* of 1966 (which, after translation in 1967, had secured world sales) and speculative theologians on dogmas like original sin, the Mass as sacrifice, the real presence of Christ in the Eucharist, creation from nothing, the primacy of Peter, the virginity of Mary, the Immaculate Conception and the Assumption. In an allocution on 'Integrity of Faith the Foundation of Christian Living', given on 30th October 1968, Paul identified the negative results of biblical criticism, reductivist and selective tendencies among some theologians, adaptation of dogma to the modern mentality by 'passing over in silence, tampering or altering certain "difficult dogmas"'. These he saw as 'deviations and errors of our times'. He said that these dispositions were only acceptable, while making the presentation of doctrine more accessible, by sincerely maintaining the integrity of faith. In 1994 the *Catechism of the Catholic Church* officially superseded all previous catechisms and finally settled doctrinal definitions.

Lefebre and accusations of modernism

One who was disenchanted by post-conciliar directions was Marcel Lefebrve, Archbishop of Anthedon and formerly Vicar Apostolic of Dakar in Senegal and later of all French-speaking Africa. He attended the Council but refused to sign some of the conciliar documents. Refusing to accept the revised Roman Missal and other reforms, in 1970, with Paul's permission, he founded the Society of St Pius X and opened a traditionalist seminary at Ecône in Switzerland. Rather than calming him down, this encouraged a vehement rejection of the Council and condemnation of what he perceived as modernist elements coming from Rome. The crisis escalated in 1976 when Lefebrve accused the Catholic hierarchy of heresy. He was officially suspended *a divinis* (that is, from all priestly and episcopal powers), and he was forbidden to ordain students studying at the seminary. By this point he had acquired a large following and the Society controlled many churches, monasteries, convents and schools throughout the world, and had acquired financial support from rich and influential benefactors. After a period of reconciliation and negotiation with the Vatican, he again split with Rome during the reign of Pope John Paul II over the question of his right to ordain bishops and the autonomy of his group within the Church. After his excommunication in 1988, his movement split into those who returned to Roman obedience and those who remained committed to his schismatic course. That lay in the future, but Paul worked hard to reconcile Lefebrve, and prevent schism. Apart from this notable exception, the Church held together and visible unity was maintained.

Final years and legacy

Paul did a great deal else for which he deserves to be remembered. He carried out more reforms, some of them of significant importance. After four centuries the *Index of Forbidden Books* was abolished. A retiring age of seventy-five for bishops and priests was introduced, and no cardinal over eighty was to vote in papal elections. He initiated a reorganisation of the Curia, a task that only a curially-trained pope could achieve.

New saints and doctors

Against Anglican protest, on 25th October 1970 he canonised forty English and Welsh martyrs of the sixteenth and seventeenth centuries put to death by the State between 1535 and 1680. The group is representative of all the 357 martyrs whose causes are still in progress, these forty being drawn from the most popular among the 199 beatified in 1886. He also proclaimed St Teresa of Avila and St Catherine of Siena doctors of the Church, the first women to be so entitled.

Simplification and collegiality

Controversially, in order that its religious significance would be clearer, he did away with the more ostentatious pageantry of the papal court and clerical attire and abolished the Palatine Guard; he sold the papal tiara presented to him at his election by the people of Milan to Cardinal Francis Spellman, Archbishop of New York, for the benefit of the poor in various countries; thereafter he only wore the mitre, a papal observance that still continues. That went with the search for Christ-centred authenticity, the mood of the times and his personal taste but went against a natural desire of many of the faithful for tradition and spectacle. But perhaps Paul's most important legacy to the Church was his steady enlargement and internationalisation of the Sacred College. The Catholic Church was no longer a European entity. When he was elected it had eighty members, but by 1976 he had raised the total to 138; its Italian members were for the first time in history a small minority, and it included many representatives from the third world. In the course of fifteen years more changes were introduced in the Church that in all previous centuries combined.

What did sadden him, and what he was not prepared for, was the mass defection from the priesthood and the religious life in the years following the conclusion of the Council. Dispensations from vows were for the first time easily available and many took advantage of them. This development was one of the most disappointing consequences that Paul was compelled to face and caused him acute desolation of mind. Once more, it was a characteristic of the period.

Huge crowds continued to greet him everywhere. He told a journalist that it was the support of the common people, who flocked to Rome in their millions for the Holy Year of 1975, which gave him the confidence to go on despite mounting criticism of the latter part of his pontificate and rumours of retirement. Progressive intellectuals and theologians complained that his reforms did not go far enough; ordinary people were sometimes nonplussed by them; the orthodox and conservative were made uneasy. But most realised that beneath the shy, rather cold manner, Paul was a man deeply moved by the physical as well as the spiritual distress of mankind. 'Wherever there is suffering', he had said in his first sermon in Milan, 'or where there is injustice or legitimate aspiration for social improvement, there will be the frank and solid defence of a pastor and father.' As Bishop of Rome, Paul showed constant solicitude for the spiritual welfare of his huge diocese, visiting the parishes, especially in the poorer districts, to offer Mass and preach, and sometimes to visit the sick in their own homes, a practice that was continued by Pope John Paul II.

Joy and courage in his sufferings

Pope John's observation on Paul's likeness to Hamlet preyed on his mind a little. Others accused him of being Quixotic. He did not keep a diary but wrote personal memoranda in a fine script. In 1975, when he was seventy-eight, beginning to weary, and was seen by the world to be pessimistic and querulous, he made the following note:

> What is my state of mind? Am I Hamlet? Or Don Quixote? On the left? On the right? I don't feel I have been properly understood. I have two dominant feelings: *Superabundo gaudio*. I am filled with comfort. With all our affliction, I am overjoyed (2 *Co* 7:4).

From the heading of this note we know that the two dominant feelings in his mind were certainty and joy (*Certezza e Gioia*). In Italian culture Hamlet is the symbol of indecisiveness. 'To be or not to be' is the only Shakespearian quotation known in Italy. Don Quixote tilts at imaginary windmills. Many thought that Paul's analysis of late-twentieth-century problems was faulty - that is the substance of the Don Quixote charge. For either he was attacking the wrong targets, or he was prophetic in the strict sense that he correctly diagnosed the present and prepared for the future. Thirty years after his death many consider that his analysis of the present and anticipation of the future was prescient.

Assassination of Aldo Moro

Aldo Moro was an Italian politician and twice Prime Minister of Italy. He was one of Italy's long-serving post-war Prime Ministers and held power for more than six years. A prominent statesman and leader of the Christian

Democratic Party, he was kidnapped in Rome on 16th March 1978 as he left his home at via Pola by a militant Communist group known at the Red Brigade, led by Mario Moretti. It was a blow struck at the heart of the Italian establishment. After fifty-five days of detention, Moro was murdered in or near Rome on 9th May and his body left later that day in a parked car. He was a lifelong friend of Paul and his kidnapping and murder profoundly disturbed him. Moro's kidnap began an agony that went on for those long days and sleepless nights. On 31st March *L'Osservatore Romano* expressed the Holy See's willingness to take steps toward the solution of this 'most painful occurrence'. On 20th April Moro's family forwarded Paul a letter written by Moro that directly appealed for his help and asked him to intercede with the Italian government. Then at 9.30 on the evening of the same day he received a letter from Moro himself appealing for an exchange of political prisoners. But Paul was unable to respond as Cardinal Jean-Marie Villot, the Secretary of State, said: 'It would be interference in the affairs of another country.' A private approach by Msgr Agostino Casaroli, head of the Council for Public Affairs of the Church, to Giulio Andreotti, the Prime Minister, was met with refusal.

Don Pasquale Macchi, Paul's private secretary, recalls what happened on the night of 21st-22nd April:

> Before supper he told me how he was going to write to the Red Brigade. After the meal, the Rosary and Compline, he went to his study at 9.30pm and worked until about 11.30. He had me take this draft to Msgr Casaroli. After some thought, Msgr Casaroli suggested some slight modifications. Paul VI considered them, recollected himself in prayer and then came back to his desk. He made me read it to him.

The letter was written in Paul's own hand and photocopies were distributed to the press next morning. He retired to bed at 2.45am.

Personal intervention and appeal

In it Paul appealed in the name of Christ, described Moro as a 'decent and innocent man', and on his knees declared:

> I beg you, free Aldo Moro, simply, without conditions, not so much because of my humble and well-meaning intercession, but because he shares with you the common dignity of a brother in humanity, and because I would dare to hope that in conscience you would not want the cause of true social progress to be stained with innocent blood or tortured by superfluous suffering.

But the letter and subsequent secret negotiations were in vain. Moro's fate had already been settled and on 9th May his body was found in the boot of a red Renault halfway between the headquarters of the Christian Democrats and Communists, riddled with bullets. The Pope could not at first accept the news. He retired to his private chapel to be alone and pray.

At the memorial service on 13th May in St John Lateran, Paul, like Job, upbraided God for allowing this appalling deed to happen: 'I will give free utterance to my complaint; I will speak in the bitterness of my soul' (*Jb* 10:1). Beamed by international television, the eighty-year-old Paul VI spoke for the nation and the world. After Paul's death the Red Brigade collapsed and some repented and made their confessions to a priest. Moro's death was 'the final twist in his crown of thorns, a last purification, a proxy agony'. It had pulled him out of lethargy and given him a role no politician could fulfil. It enabled him to confide himself to God and prepare for his own death.

Final illness and death

The feast of SS Peter and Paul, 29th June 1978, was the fifteenth anniversary of his coronation. He used the occasion to sum up and say farewell. 'I have kept the faith,' he said, he reviewed his fidelity to the Church and the Second Vatican Council, and continued: 'That was my duty, to be faithful. I've done everything. Now I've finished,' concluding with the words from the Gospel: 'Lord, to whom shall we go? Thou hast the words of eternal life.' (*Jn* 6:68) His penultimate general audience in Rome was on 26th July; thereafter he retired to Castelgandolfo, for his annual villa. His last audience on 2nd August was about Christian joy. Normally heads of state were only received in the Vatican. The next day he broke with precedent and received Sandro Pertini, the newly elected Socialist President of Italy; the audience lasted for two-and-a-half hours.

Paul in his last years suffered from severe arthritis. Over the next three days he developed a high fever caused by acute cystitis which makes arthritis even more painful. At 3am on 5th August Paul summoned his chaplain, Msgr John Magee; he needed oxygen. Msgr Magee said: 'Your Holiness, should we pray together now?' Paul replied: 'Yes, but not for me, pray for the Church.' He repeated this all day. On Sunday, 6th August, the feast of the Transfiguration, Paul obeyed his doctors and did not get up. But at noon he insisted on saying the Angelus from his window, propped up in a chair, and said: 'On this great feast of the Transfiguration, I want to recite the Angelus for all the faithful of the Church.'

He retired to bed and fell into a deep sleep. At 2pm the doctor arrived and Msgr Magee sensed in the Pope a desire to say something. When asked, Paul replied, '*Caro*, a little patience.' Those were his last recorded non-liturgical words. Don Pasquale Macchi began the Mass of the Transfiguration in the private chapel next to the Pope's bedroom at 6pm. Paul held Msgr Magee's hand throughout and joined in the Latin as though concelebrating. He received Holy Communion under both kinds and, as Mass ended, he had a massive heart attack which would have thrown him out of bed had not his chaplain held his hand. As time passed Paul was heard to murmur repeatedly the Our Father. For three hours he lingered. The Secretary of State, the Substitute, the Vicar of Rome arrived; all three, and Marco Montini, a favourite nephew, came to his uncle's bedside. Cardinal Villot began the prayers for the dying, anointed him, received a murmured thanks and a weak blessing. At 9.41pm the doctor said: 'The Pope is dead.'

Paul's achievements

Paul's great achievement was to put the Catholic Church and the papacy itself in the centre of the world stage. His pontificate, following that of Pope John XXIII, had defined the papacy's new role and he had safeguarded the substance of the Catholic faith intact. 'He managed to complete the Council without dividing the Church,' wrote Peter Hebblethwaite, Paul's English biographer, summing up his achievements, 'He reformed the Roman Curia without alienating it. He introduced collegiality without ever letting it undermine his papal office. He practised ecumenism without impairing Catholic identity. In the era of Communism, he had an *Ostpolitik* that involved neither surrender nor bouncing aggressiveness. He was "open to the world" without ever being its dupe. He pulled off the most difficult trick of all: combining openness with fidelity.'

Years later the Argentinian bishops petitioned Pope John Paul II to consider the beatification of Paul VI. His later Jesuit confessor, Paulo Dezza, recognised that, since Paul's death, an ever-growing esteem and admiration for him had developed that superseded the dismissive attitudes of the last painful years of his pontificate. He knew him well through many meetings. He said in an interview in 1989:

> I believe I can say that if he was not a saint when he was elected Pope, he became one during his pontificate. I was able to witness not only with what energy and dedication he toiled for Christ and the Church, but also and above all how much he suffered for Christ and the Church. Given his natural temperament, his sufferings brought him deep inner pain, but I have always admired not only his deep inner presence and resignation, but also his constant abandonment to divine Providence.

The process for the beatification of the Servant of God Paul VI was opened by Pope John Paul II on 11th May 1993.

Bibliography

Most quotations are taken from Peter Hebblethwaite's biography, *Paul VI: The First Modern Pope*, Harper Collins, 1993. Other references come from the works cited below.

Norman Davies, *Europe: a History*, Oxford University Press, 1996.

Eamon Duffy, *Saints and Sinners: a History of the Popes,* second edition, Yale University Press, 2005.

Austin Flannery OP, *Vatican II: The Conciliar and Post-Conciliar Documents*, vols 1 & 2, Fowler Wright, 1975, 1982.

Jean Guitton, *Paul VI secret,* Desclée de Brouwer, Paris, 1979.

The Pope Speaks: Dialogues of Paul VI with Jean Guitton, Meredith Books, 1968.

Kevane, Eugene, *Creed and Catechetics: a Catechetical Commentary on the Creed of the People of God,* Christian Classics, 1978.

Hugh McLeod, ed, *World Christianities c1914-2000, Cambridge History of Christianity,* vol 9, Cambridge University Press, 2006.

John L. McKenzie SJ, *The Roman Catholic Church*, Weidenfield & Nicholson, 1969.

Giovanni Battista Montini, *The Church*, Helicon, Dublin, 1964.

Of Human Life: Encyclical letter of Pope Paul VI, Catholic Truth Society, eds 1999, 2008.

Xavier Rynne, *Letters from Vatican City: Vatican Council II, first session: background and debates,* Faber & Faber, 1963.

The Second Session: debates and decrees of Vatican Council II, 29th September to 4th December, 1963, Faber & Faber, 1964.

The Third Session: the debates and decrees of Vatican Council II, 14th September to 21st November, 1964, Faber & Faber, 1965.

The Fourth Session: the debates and decrees of Vatican Council II, 14th September to 8th December, 1965, Faber & Faber, 1966.

R. Trisco, 'Pope Paul VI', *New Catholic Encyclopedia,* vol XI, McGraw-Hill Book Company, 1966.

James Walsh SJ, ed, *The Mind of Paul VI on the Church and the World*, Geoffrey Chapman, 1964.